W9-CKI-409

REMBRANDT

REMBRANDT

HELEN DIGBY

This edition published by
Barnes and Noble, Inc.,
by arrangement with Brompton
Books Corporation

Produced by Brompton Books
Corporation
15 Sherwood Place
Greenwich, CT 06830

ISBN 1-56619-662-0

Printed in Spain

PAGE 1: *The Syndic of the Cloth Guild, Jacob van Loon, seated*, 1661-2, Rijksmuseum, Amsterdam.

PAGE 2: *Flora*, 1638, The National Gallery, London.

BELOW: *An Elephant*, c.1637, British Museum, London.

CONTENTS

INTRODUCTION

Painter, printmaker and draftsman, Rembrandt Harmensz van Rijn is one of the towering geniuses in the history of art. He was one of the most prolific artists of seventeenth-century Europe and left a huge body of work, including portraits, religious paintings, an outstanding collection of self-portraits, and over one thousand drawings.

Rembrandt was born into a prosperous mill-owning family in Leiden in 1606 and was one of nine children. His birthplace was part of the newly-created United Provinces of the northern Netherlands, a country which was emerging from 40 years of struggle against the religious and economic authority of Spain. Calvinism was the dominant religion, but tolerance was extended toward Jews and Catholics, who were permitted freedom of worship. The combination of religious freedom and the extensive trading links of Dutch merchants meant that Dutch society, particularly in Amsterdam, became increasingly cosmopolitan and attracted many immigrants. Oriental influences became fashionable, as is evident in a number of Rembrandt's paintings, as well as those of his contemporaries.

LEFT Rembrandt *Self-Portrait, with Open Mouth*, c.1628-29, pen and brown ink with gray wash on paper, 5 × 3¾ inches (12.7 × 9.5 cm), British Museum, London. Here, Rembrandt uses the bold *chiasroscuro* to good effect.

RIGHT Pieter Lastman, *Christ on the Cross*, 1616, oil on canvas, 35⅝ × 53¾ inches (90.5 × 137.5 cm), Museum het Rembrandthuis, Amsterdam. Lastman, the leading history painter in Amsterdam, was Rembrandt's second master. His works, which were notably influenced by the paintings of Elsheimer and Caravaggio, were to inspire the young artist. Rembrandt first sought to emulate and then to surpass such models.

Rembrandt was enroled in the Faculty of Letters at Leiden University in 1620, but a year later abandoned his studies and, with his parents' consent, began an apprenticeship with the painter Jacob van Swanenburgh, from whom he learnt the rudiments of his craft. Three years later he moved to Amsterdam and worked in the studio of Pieter Lastman for six months. A far more accomplished artist, Lastman was the leading history painter in Amsterdam. He was influenced by the works of the Italian artist Caravaggio (1573-1610), whose dramatically lit canvases and moody contrasts of dark and light (*chiaroscuro*) inspired artists all over Europe. Lastman had also studied the works of Adam Elsheimer (1578-1610), a German miniaturist and printmaker known for his inventive compositions and use of brilliant colors. Lastman's work combined clear definition of characters with a strong overall narrative; in addition, he used bold colors, brightly lit against a dark backdrop.

Rembrandt returned to Leiden and established his own studio in 1625, and it is clear from his earliest paintings that he emulated his former master's style. *The Stoning of Saint Stephen* (page 26) has dramatic lighting, strong colors, and a crowded composition. His work evolved considerably in the early years of his independence; he continued to paint historical subjects, especially spiritual themes, and became more interested in realism. *Tobit and Anna with the Kid* (page 32) is the first of his masterpieces; in it he establishes a poignant narrative which is unified and defined by well-balanced lighting. The paint is applied in a smooth and creamy manner, quite unlike the style of his later years, but the technique is equally effective. The lined faces of the aged Tobit and Anna have a particular immediacy, the bright eyes of Anna contrasting with the half-closed, blind eyes of Tobit.

During these years Rembrandt experimented with the employment of light on the canvas to emphasize the most important elements of a composition; it was withdrawn from one area and made to fall in another on significant images. This is well illustrated in *Christ at Emmaus* (page 30). After the Crucifixion, two of the disciples invited an unknown man to dine with them. Only when he broke bread did they recognize him as Christ. In the painting one of them remains seated, his face wide-eyed with shock; the other kneels in the shadows at Christ's feet. Christ himself is silhouetted, with the light providing an aureole behind his head; this ingenious device ensures that His identity is immediately clear to the viewer.

The Repentant Judas Returning the Thirty Pieces of Silver to the Chief Priests and the Elders (page 38) appears to be a more sophisticated painting, with a feeling of movement and energy. It is a brilliant exercise in story-telling: Judas returns his payment to the priests,

LEFT Rembrandt *The Stoning of Saint Stephen*, 1635, etching (only state), 3¾ × 3⅜ inches (9.5 × 8.5 cm), Museum het Rembrandthuis, Amsterdam. Signed at the lower Left: *Rembrandt f. 1635.*

RIGHT Jan Lievens (1607-74), *The Raising of Lazarus*, 1631, oil on canvas, 40¼ × 43¾ inches (103 × 112 cm), Museum and Art Gallery, Brighton. Signed and dated to 1631. Lievens came into close contact with Rembrandt in the late 1620s, and it appears that the two young artists may have shared a studio. The figures in this work are very similar in terms of facial type to those in Rembrandt's interpretation of the same subject.

who bribed him to reveal Christ's whereabouts, before hanging himself. Significantly, the light falls on the Scriptures, and the elders, in their richly decorated robes, are seen to be turning away from the open book. The varying reactions of the priests can be compared with the expressions on the faces of the figures at the graveside in *The Raising of Lazarus* (page 40).

The Raising of Lazarus has led many scholars to believe that Rembrandt worked alongside another formidable Dutch painter, Jan Lievens (1607-74) during the 1620s. A number of stylistic and formal links in their work suggest that they shared a studio, and although Lievens' reputation initially seems to have overshadowed Rembrandt's, their work developed in parallel. Both men painted and etched *The Raising of Lazarus* several times between 1630 and 1631, and ideas seem to have flowed between them, although it is impossible to establish a precise chronology. The faces of the figures in the two paintings are similar, as are the colors, but the compositions are different. The work of the two young artists was evaluated by a contemporary, Constantin Huygens, who was secretary and artistic advisor to the Stadtholder, Prince Frederik Hendrik of Orange. An intelligent and cultivated man, he discusses the work of the Rembrandt and Lievens in some detail in his autobiography, and was instrumental in winning Rembrandt a sizeable commission from the prince in 1632.

Many of Rembrandt's religious paintings include studies of old people, and it is a subject he returned to several times during the 1620s. His ability to depict with clarity and poignancy the effects of ageing is clear in a number of portraits, most notably *An Old Woman: "The Artist's Mother"* (page 41). There is no way of ascertaining if this really is Rembrandt's mother, as in early records the picture is simply called "a picture of an old woman." Her face is dimly illuminated and stands out from the surrounding background darkness; the varying textures of her clothes – the fur collar, and the gold embroidery on her velvet hood – are brilliantly defined, as are the lines and delicate hues of her skin. Some critics have suggested that this precise definition is

more reminiscent of the style of Rembrandt's friend and competitor Jan Lievens, and that he is the true artist.

Rembrandt painted some 60 self-portraits, the first of which dates from 1628. His early self-portraits may have been a sign of his growing self-assurance, but there is probably a more practical reason behind them. Instead of paying a model, Rembrandt used his own face to experiment with expression, artistic techniques and lighting. His 1628 self-portrait (page 34) shows his face in shadow, a device that makes it appear three-dimensional, and his 1630 etching, *Self-Portrait, Open-mouthed*, was probably used as part of the pictorial repertoire of facial distortion which he later reused in history paintings. He appears more formal, even haughty, in the Mauritshuis *Self-Portrait* (page 35), and the fine silks and velvet of his clothes in *Self-Portrait at the Age of Thirty-Four* (page 75), were probably intended as a statement about the prestige of his profession.

Far more lucrative were commissioned portraits, and after settling in Amsterdam in 1631 Rembrandt's career altered quite radically. By this time, thanks to Huygens, he had already come to the attention of the Court, and it seemed logical to move to a larger city where he could profit from the demand for his work. He invested the considerable sum of 1000 guilders in the business of Hendrick Uylenburgh, an art dealer. The son of a cabinet maker to the king of Poland, and himself a shrewd businessman, Uylenburgh established himself as an art dealer in Amsterdam in the 1620s and provided studios for young painters.

Rembrandt's style changed after his arrival in Amsterdam; he moved away from the meticulous technique of the fine painters (*fijnschilders*) like Lievens,

LEFT Rembrandt *Bust of an Old Man in a Fur Cap*, 1630, oil on wood, 8⅝ × 6⅞ inches (22.2 × 17.7 cm), Tiroler Landesmuseum Ferdinandeum, Innsbruck. Signed: *RHL 1630*.

toward a freer, bolder style, ideally suited to portraiture. Rembrandt had not produced many portraits during the Leiden years, but the demand for such works in Amsterdam and The Hague was considerable. More than 40 of his portraits are dated 1632 or 1633, so his work was evidently extremely popular. The portraits of the 1630s, commissioned by the richer merchants, civic leaders and members of the Court, reflected the prosperity of the period, with their warm tones and glittering textiles. *Philips Lucasz* (page 61) is typical. Appointed Councillor Extraordinary to the Dutch East Indies in 1631, Lucasz was clearly a man of substance and stares imperiously out of the portrait, his gold chain of office glistening on his black jacket.

The work that really established Rembrandt's reputation, however, was *The Anatomy Lesson of Dr Nicolaes Tulp* (page 46). This was a prestigious painting commissioned to record Tulp's appointment as the first Professor of Anatomy in Amsterdam's new university. Group portraits had been common in Holland for over a century, and painting the dissection of a corpse was not an innovation either. The naturalism and animation Rembrandt brought to a traditional subject, however, was quite new. He conformed to the accepted standards of group portraits, while at the same time dazzling the viewer with a work that was, in many ways, quite unconventional. As was traditional, the faces of the members of the surgeons' guild are all clearly visible, yet unlike other groups, the subjects are actually bending over the corpse rather than being stiffly posed around it. The painting would have been seen by members of academic, political and artistic circles in Amsterdam and did a great deal to promote Rembrandt's career.

Rembrandt's most successful years coincided with the happiest phase of his personal life. He married Saskia van Uylenburgh, the cousin of the art dealer, in 1634,

RIGHT: Rembrandt *Head of an Oriental with a Bird of Paradise*, *c.*1634-35, pen and brown ink heightened with white on paper, 7 × 6⅝ inches (17.8 × 16.9cm), Cabinet des Dessins, Louvre, Paris. The white heightning over brown washes and intricate penwork gives an effective impression of the rich textures of the man's clothes.

BELOW: Rembrandt *Ledikant*, 1646, etching (fourth state), 4⅞ × 8¾ inches (12.5 × 22.4cm), Bibliothèque Nationale, Paris. Erotic themes became more prominent in Rembrandt's work during the 1640s, culminating in this tender scene.

LEFT Rembrandt *Nicolaes Ruts* (1573-1638), 1631, oil on mahogany panel, 46 × 34⅜ inches (116.8 × 87.3 cm), The Frick Collection, New York, New York. The sitter, here depicted at the age of 58, was a merchant from Cologne who had settled in Amsterdam.

and she appears in a number of his works, most notably *Flora* (1635, page 60). She is depicted as the goddess of fertility, an appropriate conceit at the start of their married life, although ironically, only the youngest of their four children, Titus, actually survived infancy. The vicissitudes of childbirth weakened Saskia and she died in 1641. She appears to have aged quickly over a short period of time; the vivacious young girl of the tender 1633 drawing has become a saddened, careworn woman by the time of *Saskia Sitting by a Window* in 1638.

Many of Rembrandt's most delightful drawings and etchings date from this period. The *Portrait of Titia van Uylenburgh* (page 72) depicts his sister-in-law peering at her needlework with her glasses perched on the end of her nose. The relaxed mood of this everyday scene contrasts with the opulence and assurance of his painted works of the same time. By their very nature, his etchings seem less formal than his paintings, but Rembrandt produced etchings as works of art in their own right, rather than regarding them as mere preparatory sketches for oil paintings. He summoned up the Dutch countryside with a few sure strokes of his pen (see *View of Amsterdam*, page 74), but he was also capable of producing complex, detailed and awe-inspiring pieces like *The Three Crosses* (page 92). He constantly re-worked his etchings, altering the composition (as he did with *Ecce Homo*, page 99) and honing the drawing until he was satisfied. These two works deal with subjects of monumental religious significance, but he could also convey an altogether

ABOVE Rembrandt *The Song of Simeon*, 1631, oil on wood, 23¾ × 18⅝ inches (60.9 × 47.8 cm), The Mauritshuis, The Hague. Simeon holds the infant Christ, and calls out in celebration.

different mood, while sticking to a liturgical theme. *St Jerome in an Italian Landscape* (page 93) is a pastoral scene, a study of the saint sunning himself after pulling a thorn from a lion's paw, and the mood is far more informal and relaxed.

Marriage to Saskia brought a degree of social advancement for Rembrandt. The van Uylenburghs were professional people, rather than traders, and fortunately the artist's fame and popularity ensured a substantial improvement in their material circumstances. He not only enjoyed the patronage of many members of the Court, but also of the Stadtholder himself. Between 1632 and 1646 Rembrandt executed seven scenes from the life and Passion of Christ for Prince Frederik Hendrick which ostensibly form a series, but as they were completed over a 14-year period, they reflect the stylistic changes evident in his work.

In the same years Rembrandt produced some of his most dramatic and challenging history paintings, such as *The Capture and Blinding of Samson* (page 64) and *Belshazzar's Feast* (page 66). Baroque influences are strong in both these works, and he was obviously inspired by Caravaggio, particularly in *Belshazzar's Feast*, where the movement, rich costumes and selective lighting capture a moment of high drama. His interest in exotic costume is apparent and was obviously fashionable. *Man in Oriental Costume ("The Noble Slav")*

ABOVE Rembrandt *Rembrandt's Mother, Full Face*, 1628, etching (state 2), 2⅜ × 2½ inches (6.3 × 6.4 cm), British Museum, London. Signed center left: *RHL 1628*.

LEFT Rembrandt *Self-Portrait with Saskia*, 1636, etching (state 1), 4 × 3¾ inches (10.4 × 9.5 cm), British Museum, London.

of 1632 (page 44) is an early example, and his interest emerged in drawings of the mid-1630s, such as *Head of an Oriental with a Bird of Paradise* (page 11).

It was in 1642, the year of Saskia's death, that Rembrandt painted what is probably his most famous work, *The Night Watch* (page 78). This painting marks the high point both of the Dutch tradition of civic guard portraits, and of Rembrandt's experiments with this genre. Following the success of *The Anatomy Lesson of Dr Nicolaes Tulp*, Rembrandt again showed great originality in breaking away from an orthodox style of portraiture by making a pictorial drama out of an everyday event. In doing so, he subordinated the individual portraits of the members of the watch to the overall demands of the painting's composition; it is almost as if he combined portraiture with history

ABOVE Rembrandt *An Old Man with a Flowing Beard; the Head Bowed Forward*, 1630, etching (only state), 35½ × 29⅝ inches (91 × 76 cm), Museum het Rembrandthuis, Amsterdam. Signed at top right: *RHL 1630.*

RIGHT Rembrandt *Saskia Sitting by a Window*, c.1638, pen and brown wash with white highlights on prepared paper 6⅞ × 5¼ inches (17.5 × 13.4 cm), Rijkmuseum, Amsterdam.

LEFT Rembrandt *The Resurrection of Christ*, 1635-39, oil on canvas, 37⅞ × 26⅛ inches (91.9 × 67 cm), Alte Pinakothek, Munich.

painting. He created a vivid, animated spectacle, a dramatically lit celebration of civic pride. It is a huge canvas, and since its recent cleaning, it is clear that *The Company of Frans Banning Cocq Preparing to March Out* (the painting's full title) is definitely not a night patrol; the nocturnal title seems to have been used first in the eighteenth century and derived from the deep shadows of the painting.

The Night Watch was highly acclaimed, yet some historians believe that it was criticized by traditionalists, who disliked the unorthodox nature of the portrait. It is probably fair to say that it won Rembrandt respect and admiration, if not complete acceptance. He was accused of painting 'too much to please himself,' something that was regarded with suspicion by lesser artists dependent on commissions for their livelihood. However, there was certainly no decline in demand for his work, and despite his personal misfortunes the quality of his paintings remained superb.

Saskia died in June 1642 at the age of 30, only 10 months after the birth of their sole surviving child, Titus. She left Rembrandt a life interest in her fortune of 40,000 guilders, which he was to forfeit if he remarried. During the late 1640s Rembrandt employed a nurse to look after his young son, a woman called Geerte Dircx. She became his lover, but they quarreled and she sued the artist for breech of promise, eventually securing a settlement of 160 guilders a year (far more than

RIGHT Rembrandt *Two Studies of Old Men's Heads*, *c.*1639, pen and brown ink on paper, 3⅛ × 3⅝ inches (8.1 × 9.4 cm), British Museum, London.

BELOW Rembrandt *The Windmill*, 1641, etching (only state), 5⅝ × 8⅛ inches (14.5 × 20.8 cm), Museum het Rembrandthuis, Amsterdam.

LEFT Johan Martinus Anthon Rieke (1851-99), *View of the Rembrandt House in Amsterdam*, 1868, pencil and pen with brown ink and watercolor heightened with white, 13½ × 7⅜ inches (34.6 × 19 cm), Museum het Rembrandthuis, Amsterdam. This is the impressive town house into which Rembrandt and his wife Saskia van Uylenburgh moved in 1639.

RIGHT Rembrandt *The Lamentation over the Dead Christ*, *c.*1635, oil on paper and canvas mounted on oak, 12½ × 10½ inches (31.9 × 26.7 cm), The National Gallery, London. Christ has been brought down from the cross and is mourned over by the Virgin on whose lap his head rests. The Magdalen clasps his feet. Golgotha is here set before an imaginary view of Jerusalem. The areas at the top and the bottom of the composition (from the horizontal of the cross facing the viewer upwards, and the feet of the Virgin down) were not painted by Rembrandt.

Rembrandt had offered). Her replacement, Hendrickje Stoffels, remained with Rembrandt until her death in 1663, and was his wife in all but name, producing a daughter, Cornelia, in 1654. Both Hendrickje and Geerte, it seems, posed as models for him, but it is hard to identify precise likenesses as there are no portraits whose original title names them as the subjects.

One woman, thought to be Hendrickje, reappears in paintings of the 1650s. There is an affectionate portrayal in a 1659 painting now known as *Portrait of Hendrickje Stoffels* (page 110) as well as *Woman at an Open Door* (page 109). The latter is a three-quarter length portrait of a woman, dressed in what appears to be luxurious night clothes. She wears gold earrings, a wedding ring

LEFT Rembrandt *Self-Portrait Drawing at a Window*, 1648, etching (drypoint and burin) (state 2), 6¼ × 5 inches (16 × 13 cm), British Museum, London. The etching is signed at the upper left: *Rembrandt. f. 1648.*

RIGHT Rembrandt *The Angel Appearing to the Shepherds*, 1634, etching (burin and drypoint) (state 3), 10¼ × 8½ inches (26.2 × 21.8 cm), British Museum, London.

and another ring on a ribbon around her neck; the marital significance of such jewelry may be important, as Rembrandt and Hendrickje never married and Hendrickje was vilified by her church in 1654 for her association with the artist.

Rembrandt also painted his son Titus many times. *Titus at his Desk* (page 101), painted in 1654, is an outstanding study of a schoolboy contemplating his studies, or simply daydreaming. The foreground of the painting is filled by the wooden grain of the desk, an extravagantly worked area with an almost abstract appeal in itself.

There are several depictions of the Holy Family dating from the 1640s which emphasize the theme of ideal domesticity. *The Holy Family with a Painted Frame and Curtain* (page 84) shows the Virgin cuddling a tired and fractious Christ Child beside a fire, with a cat curled next to them and Joseph in the shadows working on a piece of carpentry. Similarly, *The Holy Family in the Carpenter's Workshop* (page 80) has two women playing with the baby, while Joseph works contentedly alongside them. Both depict private family moments; indeed, they could be any family, but for the presence of the carpenter. The etching of *The Virgin and Child with Snake* (page 98) is another variation on this theme, but the religious significance is more immediate. The Virgin cradles Christ in front of a window, with the light streaming through a round pane of glass behind their heads, providing an aureole.

Such cosy domestic scenes were something of a contrast to his own personal life, but Rembrandt was single-minded in his ability to continue his work without either respite or a discernible decline in quality. His wife's death, the threat of financial disaster throughout the 1650s, the death of his companion, and finally of his son in 1668, all failed to make any impact on his work. He seems to have immersed himself in his painting to forget his troubles and in this period produced some of

his most acclaimed paintings and etchings – *A Woman Bathing* (page 95), *Ecce Homo* (page 99) and *The Conspiracy of Claudius Civilius* (page 118), for example.

To a certain extent during the 1650s Rembrandt painted, as his critics suggested, to please himself, and produced fewer commissioned works. His reputation, however, grew during this period. Despite his reduced circumstances, he continued to be a highly respected figure, with his fame spreading across Europe. In 1653 Don Antonio Ruffo, a Sicilian aristocrat and connoisseur, commissioned him to produce a painting of 'a philosopher.' The result was *Aristotle Contemplating the Bust of Homer*, a painting which earned Rembrandt two further commissions from Ruffo, one of which was the remarkable *A Man in Armor* (page 103). He received a sizeable fee for his work, and this, together with the

LEFT Rembrandt *Homer Dictating to a Scribe*, 1663, oil on canvas, 77⅜ × 32⅛ inches (198 × 82.4 cm), The Mauritshuis, The Hague. This is the third work Rembrandt produced for Don Antonio Ruffo.

RIGHT Rembrandt *A Young Woman Sleeping (Hendrickje Stoffels)*, c.1654, brush and brown wash on paper, 9½ × 8 inches (24.6 × 20.3 cm), British Museum, London.

proceeds from the company established by Titus and Hendrickje in 1660, kept Rembrandt's creditors at bay.

The portraits of the latter half of his career show an incredible emotional depth, and perhaps the finest example is that of *Jan Six* (page 91). Painted in 1654 to celebrate the sitter's wedding, it is an ingenious and brilliant portrait. The composition, the bold brushstrokes, the vibrant red of the cloak, and the suggestion of movement as the subject pulls on his gloves, contribute to a work of exceptional quality. The self-portraits from 1640 show similar traits and expand on earlier themes, varying between the painter as a flamboyant, prestigious craftsman (pages 75 and 111) and more serious introspective studies. He stares out of his self-portraits of the 1650s and 1660s (pages 102, 108, 113, and 114) with weary eyes, a man with no illusions, but a good deal of self-knowledge. These pictures are the culmination of a series of self-portraits which are without parallel in the history of art.

Another feature of his later works is their simplicity of composition. His paintings are less crowded, yet possess a grandeur rarely found in his earlier works. His last group portrait, *The Sampling Officers of the Cloth Makers' Guild*, also known as "The Syndics", (page 120), was painted in 1661-62. The success of this painting lies in the postures and expressions of the subjects, as well as the extreme clarity of the light. The quizzical expressions on the officers' faces give the impression that the viewer has just entered the room and interrupted the meeting.

The couple in *The Jewish Bride* (page 122) fill the canvas, in a simple yet powerful composition. The man has his arm around his wife, a protective, affectionate gesture which also gives the painting a natural border. There is nothing in the dark background to detract from this charming scene, and the tenderness of the couple seems to be enhanced by the rich, warm textures and tones of their clothes. Vincent van Gogh was so overcome by this painting that he said he would give up ten years

ABOVE Rembrandt *Lucretia*, 1666, oil on canvas, 41⅜ × 36⅓ inches (105.1 × 95.3 cm), The William Hood Dunwoody Fund, Institute of Art, Minneapolis, Minneapolis. Lucretia was a victim of rape who could not live with her perceived shame, and so committed suicide.

RIGHT Rembrandt *A Farm seen through Trees on the Bank of a River*, *c*.1650-3, reed pen and black ink with gray wash on paper washed brown, 6⅜ × 9⅛ inches (16.2 × 23.4 cm), British Museum, London.

BELOW Rembrandt *Lion Lying Down*, late 1640s, pen and brown ink with brown wash on paper, 5⅜ × 8 inches (13.8 × 20.4 cm), Cabinet des Dessins, Louvre, Paris. Rembrandt and some of his pupils made a number of studies of lions which were imported to the United Provinces from North Africa by the East India Company.

of his life just to be allowed to sit in front of it for a fortnight.

When Rembrandt died in 1669, he was poor and his paintings unpopular, and it was not until the eighteenth century that his work again became praised and much-imitated. It is not only the quality (and sheer quantity) of his oeuvre which set him apart from his contemporaries, but also its diversity. Most of his peers specialized in one particular genre, but from the earliest days of his career, Rembrandt showed that he was equally good at history paintings, or portraits and is acknowledged as the finest etcher in the history of art. He was also an excellent teacher. He took his first pupil, Gerard Dou in 1628 and Aert de Gelder, whom he taught at the end of his life in the 1660s, continued his style into the eighteenth century.

ABOVE
The Stoning of Saint Stephen, 1625
Oil on wood, 35 × 48¼ inches (89.5 × 123.6 cm)
Museé des Beaux-Arts, Lyon.

RIGHT
The Music Party, 1626
Oil on wood, 24¾ × 18½ inches (63.4 × 47.6 cm)
Rijksmuseum, Amsterdam.
Signed and dated: *RH. 1626*

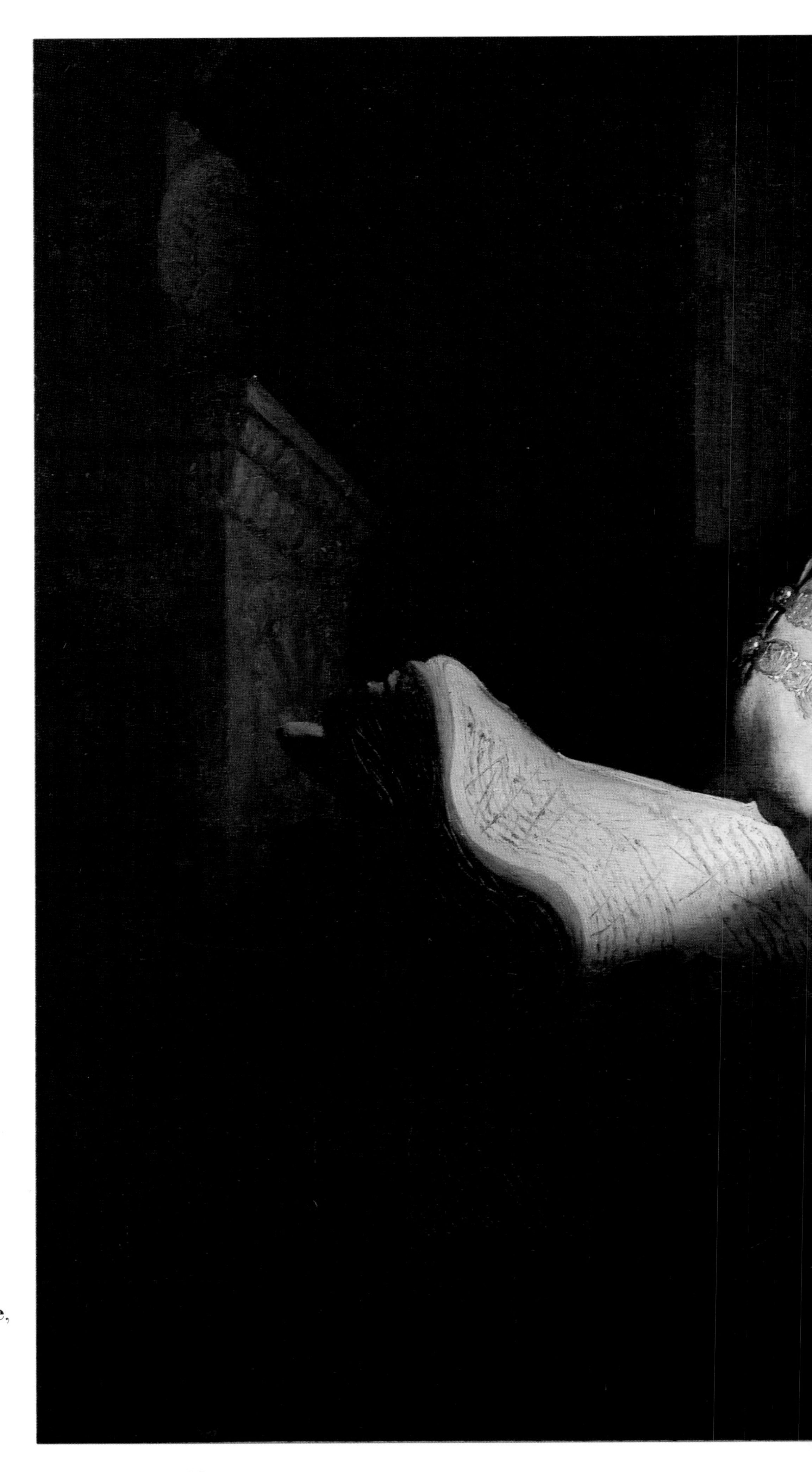

The Rich Man from the Parable, 1627
Oil on wood, 12½ × 16⅝ inches (31.9 × 42.5 cm)
Gemäldegalerie, Berlin.
Signed and dated: *RH. 1627*

Christ at Emmaus, *c.*1628
Oil on paper stuck to wood, 14⅝ × 16½ inches (37.4 × 42.3 cm)
Museé Jacquemart-Andre, Paris.

ABOVE
Two Old Men Disputing, 1628
Oil on wood, 28¼ × 23¼ inches (72.3 × 59.6 cm)
Felton Bequest, National Gallery of Victoria, Melbourne.

LEFT
Tobit and Anna with the Kid, 1626
Oil on wood, 15⅝ × 11⅝ inches (40.1 × 29.9 cm),
Rijksmuseum, Amsterdam.
Signed and dated: *RH. 1626*

ABOVE
Self-Portrait, *c.*1628
Oil on wood, 8¾ × 7¼ inches (22.5 × 18.6 cm)
Rijksmuseum, Amsterdam.

RIGHT
Self-Portrait, *c.*1629
Oil on wood, 14¾ × 11¼ inches (37.9 × 28.9 cm)
The Mauritshuis, The Hague.

The Artist in His Studio, *c.*1629
Oil on wood, 9¾ × 12½ inches (25.1 × 31.7 cm)
Zoe Oliver Sherman Collection.
Given in memory of Lillie Oliver Poor.
Museum of Fine Arts, Boston, Massachusetts.

The Repentant Judas Returning the Thirty Pieces of Silver to the Chief Priests and Elders, 1629
Oil on wood, 30⅝ × 40 inches (79 × 102.3 cm)
Private collection, England.

ABOVE

The Raising of Lazarus, *c.*1630

Oil on wood, 37 15/16 × 32 inches (96.2 × 81.5 cm)

Gift of H R Ahmanson & Co., in memory of Howard F Ahmanson, Los Angeles County Museum of Art, Los Angeles, CA.

RIGHT

An Old Woman: "The Artist's Mother", *c.*1629

Oil on wood, 23 5/8 × 18 1/2 inches (61 × 47.4 cm)

Royal Collection, Windsor Castle,

Jeremiah Lamenting the Destruction of Jèrusalem, 1630
Oil on wood, 22¾ × 18¼ inches (58.3 × 46.6 cm)
Rijksmuseum, Amsterdam.

The Prophetess Anna, 1631
Oil on wood, 23⅜ × 18⅝ inches (59.8 × 47.7 cm)
Rijksmuseum, Amsterdam.

ABOVE
Man in Oriental Costume ("The Noble Slav"), 1632
Oil on canvas, 60⅛ × 43¾ inches (152.7 × 111.1 cm)
Bequest of William K Vanderbilt, 1920
Metropolitan Museum of Art, New York.

RIGHT
An Old Man in Military Costume, *c.*1631
Oil on wood, 26 × 20 inches (66 × 50 cm)
J Paul Getty Museum, Malibu, CA.

Rembrandt
f

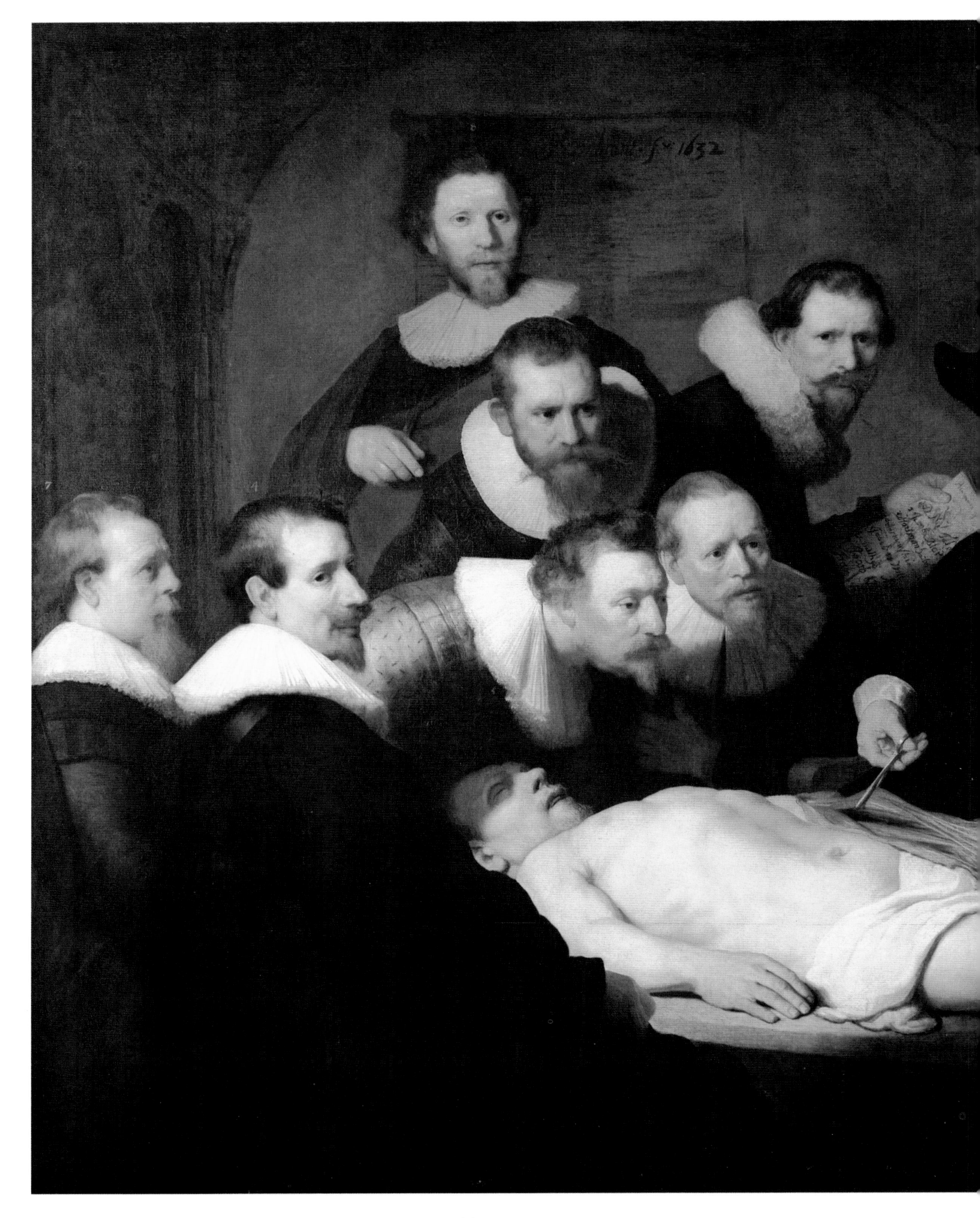

The Anatomy Lesson of Dr Nicolaes Tulp, 1632
Oil on canvas, 66¼ × 84½ inches (169.5 × 216.5 cm)
The Mauritshuis, The Hague.

Jan Rijksen (1560/61-1637) and Griet Jans (*c.* 1560-after 1653), 1633
Oil on canvas, 44⅝ × 66 inches (114.3 × 168.9 cm)
HM Queen Elizabeth II, Buckingham Palace.

ABOVE
Frederick Rihel on Horseback, *c.*1633
Oil on canvas, 115 × 94⅞ inches (294.5 × 241 cm)
The National Gallery, London.

RIGHT
The Raising of the Cross, *c.*1633
Oil on canvas, 37½ × 28¼ inches (96.2 × 72.2 cm)
Alte Pinakothek, Munich.

ABOVE

Christ in the Storm on the Sea of Galillee, 1633

Oil on canvas, 63 × 50 inches (162 × 130 cm)

Isabella Stewart Gardner Museum, Boston, Massachusetts.

Signed: *Rembrandt f. 1633.*

RIGHT

The Descent from the Cross, *c.*1633

Oil on wood 34⅞ × 25½ inches (89.4 × 65.2 cm)

Alte Pinakothek, Munich.

ABOVE
Saint John the Baptist Preaching, *c.*1634
Oil on canvas laid on panel, 24¼ × 31¼ inches (62 × 80 cm)
Staatliche Museen Preussischer Kulturbesitz, Gemäldegalerie, Berlin.

LEFT
The Holy Family, *c.*1634
Oil on canvas, 71⅝ × 48 inches (183.5 × 123 cm)
Alte Pinakothek, Munich.

ABOVE
The Lamentation at the Foot of the Cross,
*c.*1634-35
Pen and ink and wash with chalk, reworked in oil,
8½ × 9 inches (21.6 × 25.4 cm)
British Museum, London.

RIGHT
Portrait of an Eighty-Three-year-old Woman,
1634
Oil on wood, 27¾ × 21⅝ inches (71.1 × 55.9 cm)
The National Gallery, London.
Signed and dated: *Rembrandt f.1634*

Ecce Homo, 1634
Oil on paper stuck on canvas, 21¼ × 17⅜ inches
(54.4 × 44.5 cm)
The National Gallery, London.
Signed beneath the clock at the right: *Rembrandt.f./1634*

The Death of the Virgin, 1639
Etching (drypoint) (state 1), 16 × 12¼ inches (40.9 × 31.5 cm)
British Museum, London.

ABOVE
Flora, 1635
Oil on canvas, 48¼ × 38 inches (123.5 × 97.5 cm)
The National Gallery, London.

RIGHT
Philips Lucasz, 1635
Oil on wood, 31 × 23 inches (79.5 × 58.9 cm)
The National Gallery, London.
Signed: Rembrandt/1635

LEFT
The Rape of Ganymede, 1635
Oil on canvas, 66¾ × 50¾ inches (171 × 30 cm)
Gemäldegalerie, Dresden.

BELOW
Danaë, 1636
Oil on canvas, 64½ × 79¼ inches (185 × 203 cm)
The Hermitage, St Petersburg.

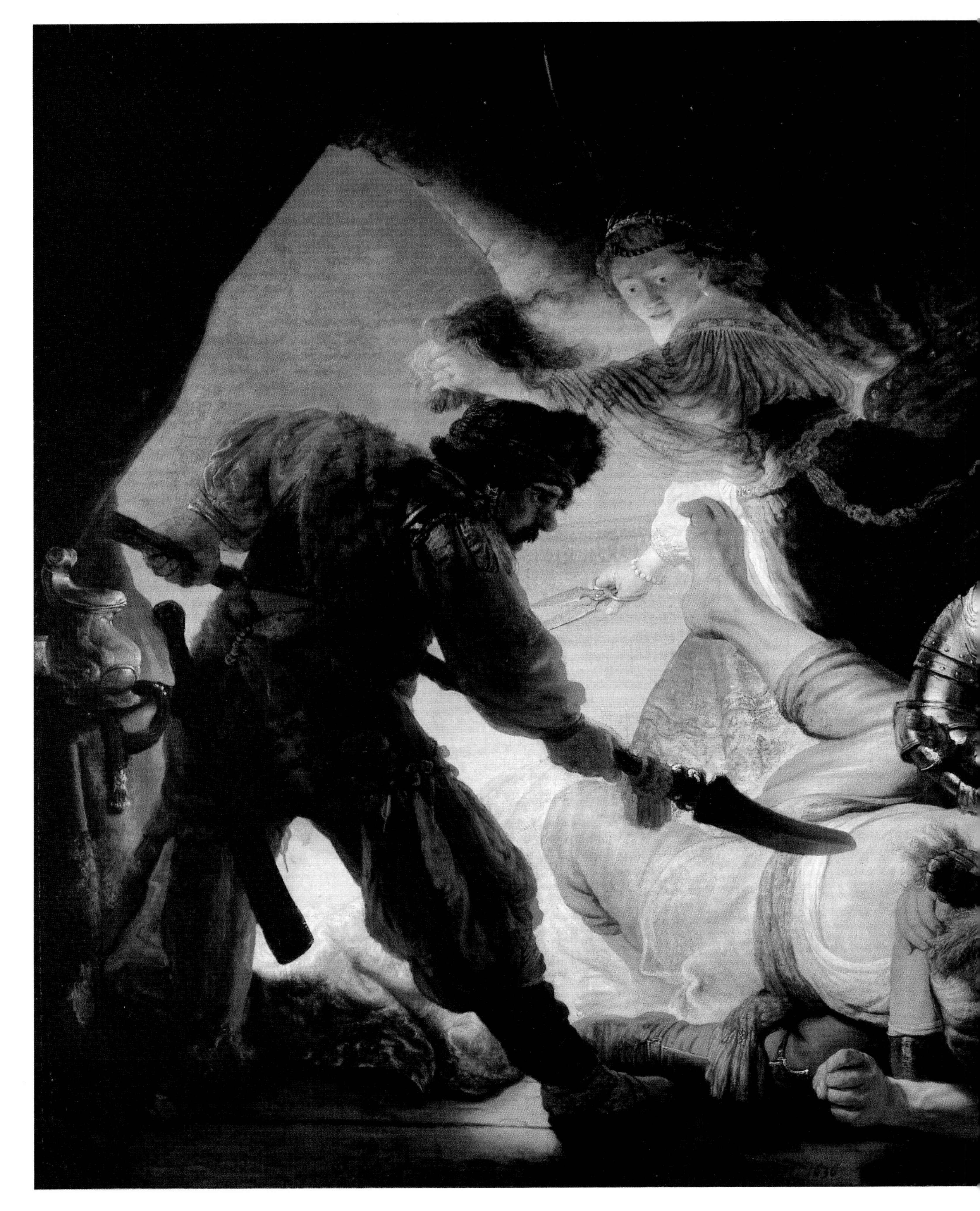

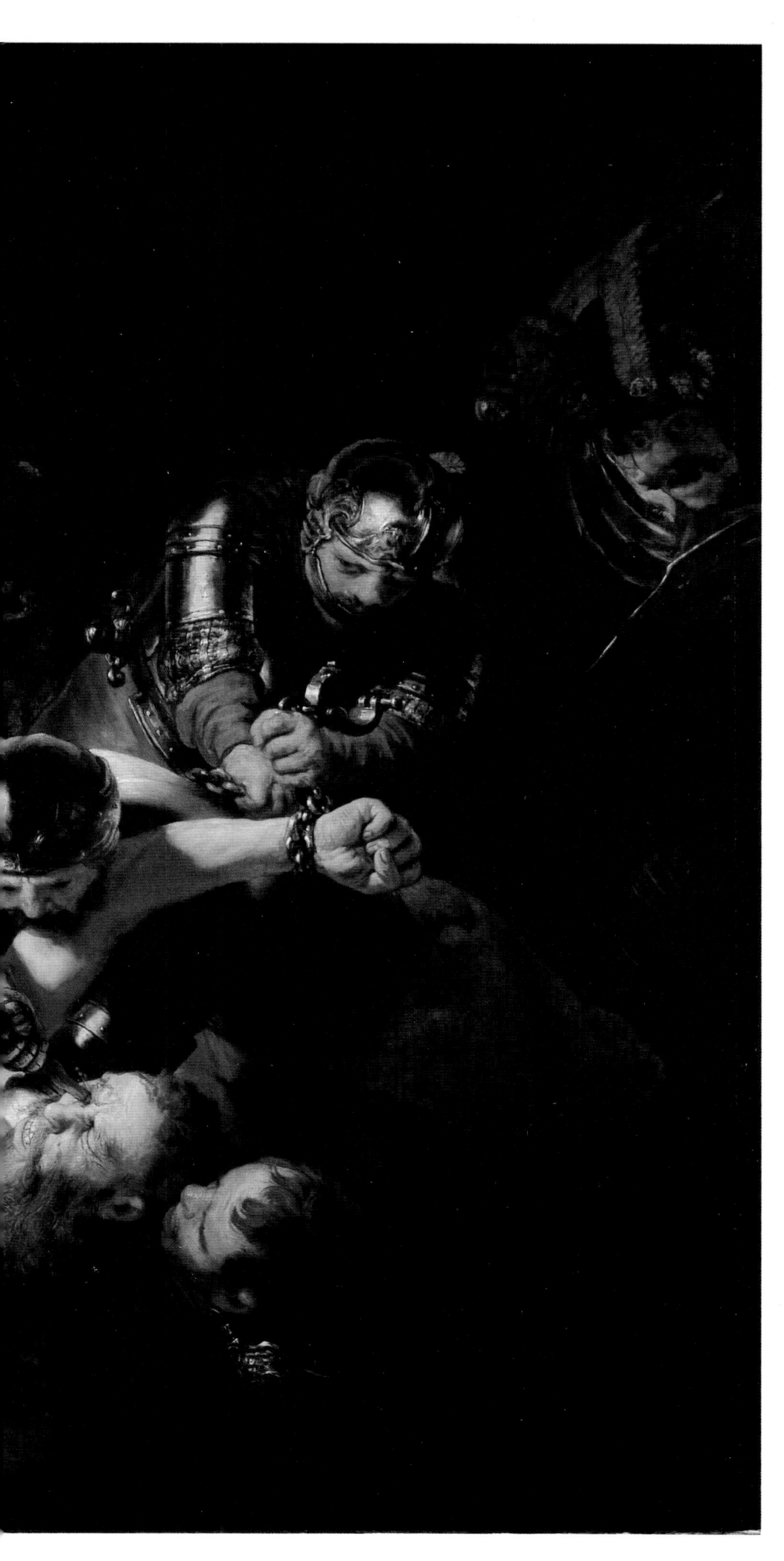

The Capture and Blinding of Samson, 1636
Oil on canvas, 80 × 106¼ inches (205 × 272 cm)
Städelsches Kunstinstitut, Frankfurt.

Belshazzar's Feast, *c.*1636-38
Oil on canvas, 65½ × 81¾ inches (167.6 × 209.2 cm)
The National Gallery, London.

ABOVE
Landscape with a Stone Bridge, *c.*1638
Oil on wood, 11½ × 16⅝ inches (29.5 × 42.5 cm)
Rijksmuseum, Amsterdam.

LEFT
The Angel Leaving Tobias and His Family, 1637
Oil on panel, 26½ × 20¼ inches (68 × 52 cm)
Louvre, Paris.
Signed: *Rembrandt f.1637.*

ABOVE
The Risen Christ Appearing to Mary Magdalen, 1638
Oil on wood, 23⅝ × 19⅜ inches (61 × 49.5 cm)
HM Queen Elizabeth II, Buckingham Palace.
Signed: *Rembrandt f. 1638*

RIGHT
Portrait of a Man Standing, 1639
Oil on canvas, 78¼ × 48½ inches (200 × 124.5 cm)
Gemäldegalerie, Kassel.

Portrait of Titia van Uylenburgh, 1639
Nationalmuseum, Stockholm.

Still Life with Two Dead Peacocks and a Girl,
*c.*1639
Oil on canvas, 56⅝ × 52⅞ inches (145 × 135.5 cm)
Rijksmuseum, Amsterdam.

View of Amsterdam, *c.*1640
Etching (only state), 4³⁄₈ × 6 inches (11.2 × 15.3 cm)
Museum het Rembrandthuis, Amsterdam.

Self-Portrait at the Age of Thirty-Four, 1640
Oil on canvas, 39⅞ × 31¼ inches (102 × 80 cm)
The National Gallery, London.
Signed and dated: *Rembrandt f.1640*

Portrait of Agatha Bas, 1641
Oil on canvas, 41 × 32¾ inches (105.2 × 83.9 cm)
HM Queen Elizabeth II, Buckingham Palace.

The Flute Player, 1642
Etching (drypoint) (state 3), 4½ × 5⅝ inches
(11.6 × 14.3 cm)
British Museum, London.

The Company of Frans Banning Cocq Preparing to March Out, known as "The Night Watch", 1642
Oil on canvas, 141¾ × 170¾ inches (363 × 437 cm)
On loan from the City of Amsterdam to the Rijksmuseum, Amsterdam.

ABOVE
The Holy Family in the Carpenter's Workshop, *c.*1645
Pen with brown ink and wash touched with white on paper, 7¼ × 9⅝ inches (18.4 × 24.6 cm)
British Museum, London.

RIGHT
The Woman Taken in Adultery, 1644
Oil on wood, 32½ × 25⅛ inches (83.3 × 64.4 cm)
The National Gallery, London.

Girl Leaning on a Windowsill, 1645
Oil on canvas, 31⅞ × 25¾ inches (81.6 × 66 cm)
Dulwich Picture Gallery, London.

The Adoration of the Shepherds, 1646
Oil on canvas, 25½ × 21½ inches (65.5 × 55 cm)
The National Gallery, London.

The Holy Family with a Painted Frame and Curtain, 1646
Oil on wood, 18⅛ × 26⅞ inches (46.5 × 68.8 cm)
Gemäldegalerie, Kassel.

Susanna and the Elders, 1647
Oil on canvas, 29⅝ × 35½ inches (76 × 91 cm)
Staatliche Museen Preussischer Kulturbesitz, Gemäldegalerie, Berlin.

Christ at Emmaus, 1648
Oil on wood, 26½ × 25⅜ inches (68 × 65 cm)
Louvre, Paris.

Young Woman in Bed, *c.*1647
Oil on canvas, 31¾ × 26½ inches (81.3 × 68 cm)
The National Gallery of Scotland, Edinburgh.

Jan Six, 1654
Oil on canvas, 43¾ × 39⅞ inches (112 × 102 cm)
Six Collection, Amsterdam.

The Three Crosses, 1653-61
Etching (drypoint and burin) (state 4), 15 × 17½ inches (38.5 × 45 cm)
British Museum, London.

Saint Jerome in an Italian Landscape, *c.*1654
Etching (drypoint) (state 1), 10⅛ × 8¼ inches (25.9 × 21 cm)
British Museum, London.

ABOVE
Flora, *c.*1654
Oil on canvas, 39⅜ × 36⅛ inches (100 × 91.8 cm)
Gift of Archer M Huntington in memory of his father, Collis Potter Huntington, 1926
The Metropolitan Museum of Art, New York, New York.

RIGHT
A Woman Bathing, 1654
Oil on wood, 24⅛ × 18⅜ inches (61.8 × 47 cm)
The National Gallery, London.
Signed at the bottom left: *Rembrandt f 1654*

Bathsheba with King David's Letter, 1654
Oil on canvas, 55½ × 55½ inches (142 × 142 cm)
Louvre, Paris.

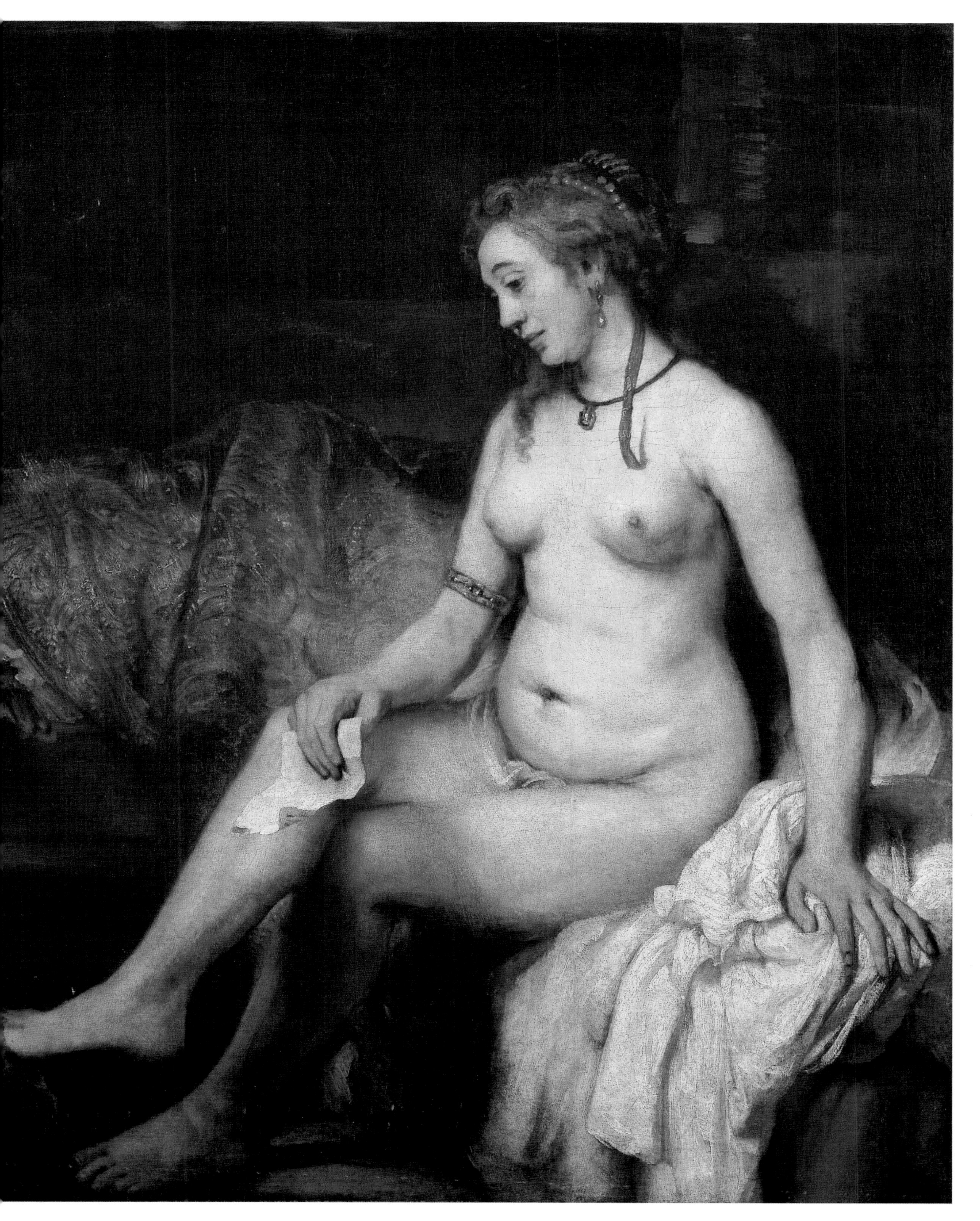

The Virgin and Child with the Snake, 1654
Etching (only state), 3¾ × 5⅝ inches (9.5 × 14.5 cm)
British Museum, London.

Ecce Homo, 1655
Etching (drypoint) (state 4), 15 × 17¾ inches
(38.3 × 45.5 cm)
British Museum, London.

An Old Woman Reading, 1655
Oil on canvas, 31¼ × 25¾ inches (80 × 66 cm)
Collection of the Duke of Buccleuch, Drumlanrig Castle, Scotland.

Titus at his Desk, 1655
Oil on canvas, 30 × 24½ inches (77 × 63 cm)
Museum Boymans-van Beuningen, Rotterdam.

ABOVE
Self-Portrait, *c.*1655
Oil on wood, 19¼ × 16 inches (49.2 × 41 cm)
Kunsthistorisches Museum, Vienna.

RIGHT
A Man in Armor, 1655
Oil on canvas, 53¾ × 40⅞ inches (137.5 × 104.5 cm)
The City Art Gallery and Museum, Glasgow.

Jacob Blessing the Sons of Joseph, 1656
Oil on canvas, 68½ × 82¼ inches
(175.5 × 210.5 cm)
Gemäldegalerie, Kassel.

The Anatomy Lecture of Dr Joan Deyman, 1656
Oil on canvas, 39 × 52³/₈ inches (100 × 134 cm)
On loan from the City of Amsterdam to the Rijksmuseum, Amsterdam.

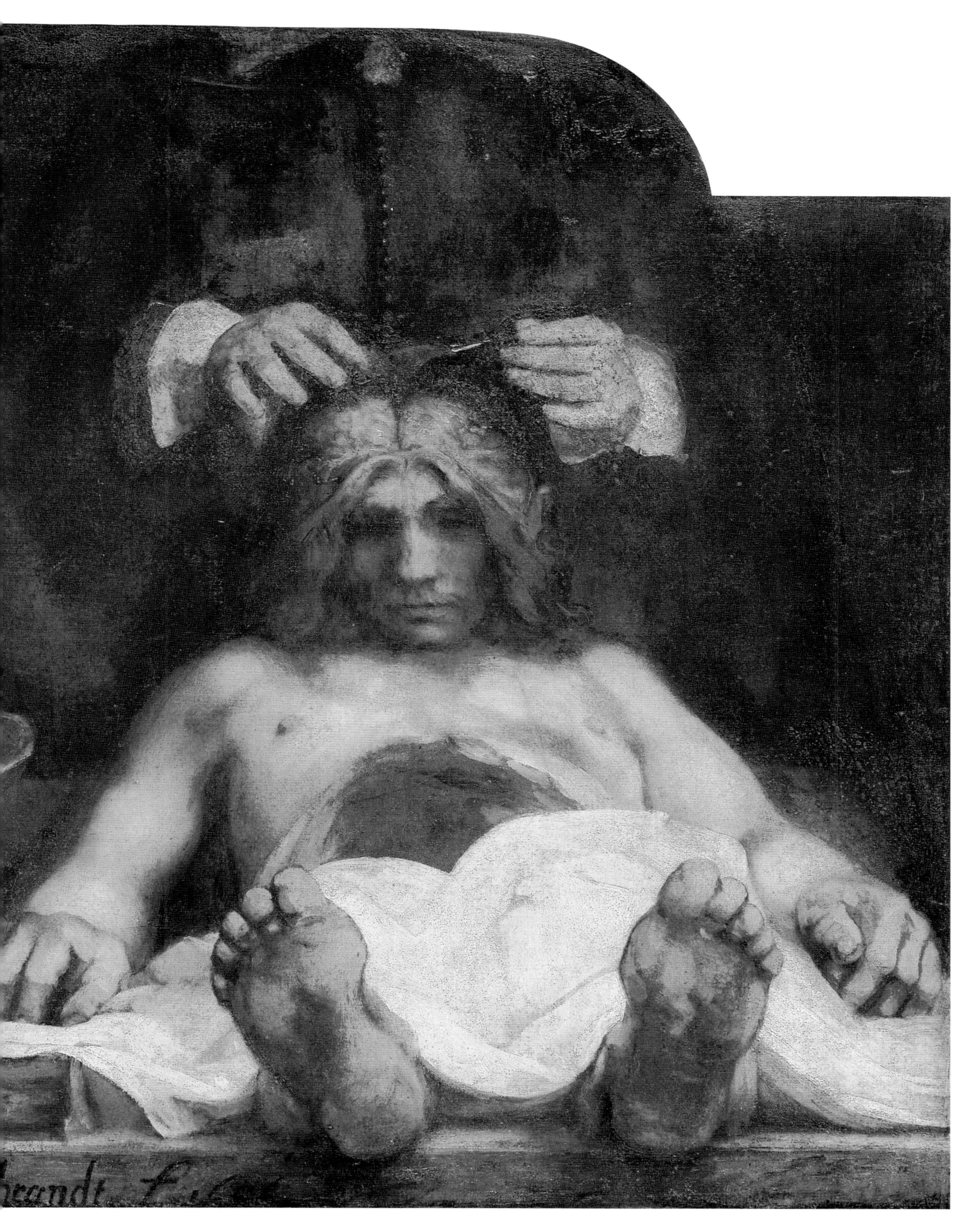

ABOVE
Self-Portrait, 1657
Oil on canvas, 20⅞ × 17⅛ inches (53.5 × 44 cm)
Collection of the Duke of Sutherland, on loan to The National Gallery of Scotland, Edinburgh.

RIGHT
Woman at an Open Door (Hendrickje Stoffels?), *c.*1656
Oil on canvas, 34½ × 26⅛ inches (88.5 × 67 cm)
Staatliche Museen Preussischer Kulturbesitz, Gemäldegalerie, Berlin.

ABOVE
Portrait of Hendrickje Stoffels, 1659
Oil on canvas, 39¾ × 32⅝ inches
(101.9 × 83.7 cm)
The National Gallery, London.

RIGHT
Self-Portrait, 1658
Oil on canvas, 52⅝ × 40⅞ inches
(133.7 × 103.8 cm)
The Frick Collection, New York, New York.

ABOVE
Juno, c.1661
Oil on canvas, 49½ × 42 inches (127 × 107.5 cm)
Armand Hammer Foundation, Los Angeles.

RIGHT
Self-Portrait, 1660
Oil on canvas
Louvre, Paris.

ABOVE
Self-Portrait as the Apostle Paul, 1661
Oil on canvas, 35½ × 30 inches (91 × 77 cm)
Rijksmuseum, Amsterdam.

RIGHT
Margaretha de Geer, 1661
Oil on canvas, 51 × 38 inches (130.5 × 97.5 cm)
The National Gallery, London.

LEFT
Jacob Trip, 1661
Oil on canvas, 51 × 37⅞ inches (130.5 × 97 cm)
The National Gallery, London.

ABOVE
Self-Portrait, *c.*1661-62
Oil on canvas, 44⅝ × 37⅛ inches (114.3 × 95.2 cm)
The Iveagh Bequest, Kenwood House, London.

The Conspiracy of Claudius Civilius, 1661-62
Oil on canvas, 76½ × 120¾ inches (196 × 309 cm)
Nationalmuseum, Stockholm.

The Sampling Officials of the Drapers' Guild ("The Syndics"), 1661
Oil on canvas, 74¾ × 109 inches (191.5 × 279 cm)
Rijksmuseum, Amsterdam.

Rembrandt f. 1661

The Jewish Bride,
*c.*1662
Oil on canvas,
47½ × 65 inches
(121.5 × 166.5 cm)
Rijksmuseum, Amsterdam.

Rembrandt f.

A Family Group, *c.*1663-68
Oil on canvas, 49¼ × 65¼ inches (126 × 167 cm)
Herzog Anton Ulrich-Museum, Braunschweig.

Self-Portrait, 1669
Oil on canvas, 33½ × 27½ inches (86 × 70.5 cm)
The National Gallery, London.

Self-Portrait, 1669
Oil on canvas, 24¾ × 22½ inches (63.5 × 57.8 cm)
The Mauritshuis, The Hague.

Acknowledgments

The author and publisher would like to thank Simon Shelmerdine for production, Martin Bristow the designer, and Judith Millidge the editor, for their help in the preparation of this book. We are grateful to the following individuals and institutions for permission to reproduce the images on the pages noted below.

Alte Pinakothek, Munich/Artothek: pages 16, 51, 54
Armand Hammer Collection, Armand Hammer Museum of Art and Cultural Center, Los Angeles: page 112
Ashmolean Museum, Oxford: page 88
Bibliothèque Nationale, Paris: page 11(bottom)
Collection of the Duke of Buccleuch and Queensberry KT, Drumlanrig Castle, Dumfries and Galloway: page 100
Courtesy of the Trustees of the British Museum: pages 4, 6, 14(both), 17(top), 20, 21, 23, 25(top), 53, 56, 79, 80, 92, 93, 98, 99
Courtesy of the Trustees of the National Gallery, London: pages 2, 18, 19, 50, 57, 58, 59, 60, 61, 66, 75, 81, 83, 95, 110, 115, 116, 126
Dulwich Picture Gallery, London: page 82
Fitzwillian Museum, Cambridge: page 74
The Frick Collection, New York: pages 12, 111
Gemäldegalerie, Museen Preussischen Kulturbesitz, Berlin: pages 28, 55, 86, 109
Gemäldegalerie, Dresden: page 62
Gemäldegalerie, Kassel: page 71, 84, 104
J Paul Getty Museum, Malibu: page 46
Glasgow Museums; Art Gallery and Museum, Kelvingrove: pages 103
Hermitage Museum, St Petersburg/Bridgeman Art Library: page 63
Herzog Anton Ulrich-Museum, Brunswick: pages 124
Isabella Stewart Gardner Museum, Boston: page 52
The Iveagh Bequest, Kenwood House, London: page 117
Kunsthitorisches Museum, Vienna: page 102
Los Angeles County Museum of Art: page 40 (Gift of H R Ahmanson and Co in memory of Howard F Ahmanson)
Mauritshuis, The Hague: pages 13, 22, 35, 46, 127
The Metropolitan Museum of Art, New York: page 44 (Bequest of William Kijk Vanderbilt, 1920), 94 (Gift of Archer M Huntington in memory of his father Collis Potter Huntington)
Minneapolis Institute of Arts: page 24 (The William Hood Dunwoody Fund)
Musée des Beaux-Arts, Lyon: page 26
Musée Jacquemart André, Paris: page 30
Musée du Louvre/Réunion des Musées Nationaux: pages 11(top) 25(below), 45, 68, 88, 96, 113
Museum Boymans-van Beunigen, Rotterdam: page 101
Museum of Fine Arts, Boston: page 36 (Zoe Oliver Sherman Collection. Given in memory of Lillie Oliver Poor).
Museum het Rembrandthuis, Amsterdam: pages 7, 8, 15(top), 17(below), 18
Museum and Art Gallery, Brighton: page 9
National Gallery of Scotland, Edinburgh: page 90, 108
National Gallery of Victoria, Melbourne: page 33
Nationalmuseum, Stockholm: page 72, 118
Private Collection: page 37
Rijksmuseum, Amsterdam: pages 1, 6, 15(below), 27, 32, 34, 41, 43, 69, 73, 78, 106, 114, 120, 122
Royal Collection, Buckingham Palace. © 1993 Her Majesty The Queen: pages 48, 70, 76
Royal Collection, Windsor Castle. © 1993 Her Majesty The Queen: page 41
Six Collection, Amsterdam: page 91
Städeslsches Kunstinstitut, Frankfurt: page 64
Tiroler Landesmuseum Ferdinandeum, Innsbruck: page 10